I am the cat, don't forget that

Also by Valerie Shaff and Roy Blount Jr.

Am I pig enough for you yet?:
  Voices of the barnyard

I am puppy hear me yap:
  The ages of dog

If only you knew how much I smell you:
  True portraits of dogs

I am the cat, don't forget that

Feline expressions

Photographs by Valerie Shaff

Text by Roy Blount Jr.

HarperCollins*Publishers*

For Elsie, and Halloween. Not Pepe. —R.B.

Lokah Samasta Sukhino Bhavantu.
May all beings, everywhere, be happy and free, and may the
thoughts and actions of our lives contribute to that happiness
and to that freedom for all. —V. S.

I AM THE CAT, DON'T FORGET THAT. Photographs copyright © 2004 by Valerie Shaff and text copyright © 2004 by Roy Blount Jr. All rights reserved. Printed in Japan. No part of this book may be used or reproduced in any manner whatsoever without written permission except in the case of brief quotations embodied in critical articles and reviews. For information, address HarperCollins Publishers Inc., 10 East 53rd Street, New York, NY 10022.

HarperCollins books may be purchased for educational, business, or sales promotional use. For information, please write: Special Markets Department, HarperCollins Publishers Inc., 10 East 53rd Street, New York, NY 10022.

FIRST EDITION

Printed on acid-free paper

Library of Congress Cataloging-in-Publication Data
Shaff, Valerie.
I am the cat, don't forget that : feline expressions / photographs by Valerie Shaff ; text by Roy Blount Jr.—1st ed.
p. cm.
ISBN 0-06-056041-X
1. Photography of cats.   2. Cats—Pictorial works.   3. Shaff, Valerie.   4. Cats—Poetry.
I. Blount, Roy.   II. Title.
TR729.C3S28 2004   2004044002
636.8'0022'2—dc22

04   05   06   07   08   ❖/TOP   10   9   8   7   6   5   4   3   2   1

Acknowledgments

I want to thank the following people for their essential contributions to the realization of this book: Roy Blount Jr., for his mastery of words that always enhances my photographs, Janis Donnaud; my editors, Larry Ashmead and Mark Bryant, and assistant editor Emily McDonald; my design and production friends, Lucy Albanese, Roni Axelrod, and John Hanley.

Some of these portraits were commissions, some were assignments, and some were simply inspirations. I am grateful to all my co-conspirators who assisted in summoning these results. Cats usually don't volunteer to be photographed as other animals do. For cat-related assignments resulting in some of my favorite portraits in this book, I'd like to thank Renee Walsh, Martha Stewart, Chris Kreback, Matt Ronken, and Yucel Erdogan.

Lastly, I'd like to take this opportunity to acknowledge and thank for her tireless efforts Katrin Hecker, founder and chief of Animalkind. There is endless work to be done to diminish the suffering of unwanted and uncared-for cats. It is a rare person who endeavors to change a situation that is endlessly challenging. Katrin is such a person.

I dedicate my work in this book to the cat lovers and activists everywhere who devote themselves to bringing awareness to, and improving the conditions for, cats struggling in our increasingly un-natural world.

—Valerie Shaff

Introduction

BY ROY BLOUNT JR.

My identification with animals comes from my mother. She preferred dogs, because they are more willing (at least our dogs were) to share complex emotional loads. Sometimes in the throes of housework she would demand of the incumbent cat or dog, "What do *you* contribute to the household?" The dog would all but scratch his or her head and whimper, "Gee . . . I . . ." The cat might yawn.

A cat will stand up to anything: physical threat (the tiniest kitten will arch its back and hiss at a bully that would make the average grown dog roll over and expose its belly), emotional blackmail, even the well-meaning intrusion of a grandparent into the home. When I visited my daughter and her family recently, their cat Pepe threw up on one of my books. It was a brand-new copy of my anthology of Southern humor, which I had autographed for a charity my daughter supports. I had left the book on Pepe's kitchen counter. My photograph on the cover, even after a cleaning, was left pointedly faded.

Cat humor. There is a book out called *Cats for Dummies*. There is no book called *Dummies for Cats*. Cats don't feel they need one.

Another time, in my own home, a cat of my own, Eloise, whom I had never treated unkindly . . .

Okay, I had disparaged her meow. Instead of going *meow*, Eloise went *wank*. Maybe I pointed this out to her once too often . . .

Early one morning, I dreamed that I had a Hitler mustache. I awoke to find Eloise standing with one foot on my upper lip.

But let me tell you a more heartwarming story. New York City, 1969. My daughter was not yet three years old. She and I and her baby brother and my first wife had two cats, Abyssinians, named Bale and Kobar. One day Bale, in a comfortable cardboard box, with Kobar pacing back and forth and occasionally peering in and muttering, delivered four kittens. The fourth-born was weak. It kept getting pushed off to one side away from Bale, where it cried in an odd voice and twitched feebly. Then Kobar and Bale began to shiver. Shivering in the mother might mean eclampsia; there was no excuse for Kobar to shiver.

We were living in Manhattan and had no car. Nor did we have a cat carrier that could accommodate six cats (two of them shivering; four of them tiny, and one of those impaired) comfortably enough that they could be carried alive on foot by one person for long. Nor did we have whatever it might take to load two adults, two small children, and six cats into and out of a taxi.

So we put Kobar in the cat carrier, and him and the two children in the baby buggy, which my wife pushed, carefully, and I carried Bale and the kittens, carefully, in the big cardboard box of the nativity, with a top on it and holes cut out for air and light. Eventually we all ten made it the twelve blocks to the vet's.

The vet prescribed a whole lot of pills and powders that would make the whole cat family right, except for the feeble kitten. He would need to have butter smeared all over him. That would induce Bale to lick him more, for stimulation.

And it worked. It felt pretty questionable, I can tell you, to smear butter, with a little calcium lactate mixed in, on a minuscule, faintly wriggling furball, but in the long run it lent him vigor. Soon the runt was tearing into the scrimmage like a tiger. Sometimes we would have to pull a larger kitten out of his way, but then he would latch on with a will and hold his own. In the process he got butter all over his siblings.

Buttered kittens. Both parents enjoyed licking them. Let's have a chorus of "Wo-oh-oh-oh-oh . . . *Fee*—lines."

But cats aren't Barry Manilow. Nor would we want them to be.

When our neighbors' cat Maude got run over in her prime by the bread man, my mother assured me that there was a cat heaven. I see it not as some minor backwater of paradise. Nothing showy, either; but elegant. Certain carefully screened people would be there, at their request. And some penitential dogs, as attendants. And birds, and mice.

I lived with a cat named Angel once. For Angel's sake there would be no umbrellas in heaven. A tatty-elegant Persian who had lived in England, Angel was terrified of umbrellas. Anytime she saw one, open or closed, she would jump out of her skin. Some nights she evidently dreamed of umbrellas, because she'd go *WAAAA*, sail out of the bed as if flung by some unseen hand, and *thump*, you'd hear her hit the wall. When the lights came on, she would deny that anything had happened.

In heaven (as in life) Mencken—a stray I found at the H. L. Mencken house, in Baltimore, and brought home with high hopes of literary companionship—would be relieving herself in bathtubs to her heart's content. I don't know that I'd want to see Mencken in the hereafter, although she was an interesting writer (see page xv). But I'd love to run into Snope again—a hearty indoor-outdoor black-and-white cat who did not share his sister Eloise's differently-abled meow.

Ah, and Emmy, the most robust cat I've known, and the fluffiest. Emmy was fluffy even on the bottoms of her feet, and she chased dogs. Whereas Lulu was a cat who belonged with Tubby, a plump Boston bull. We got them at the same time, when I was around seven, and I can't picture either of them in any way except rolling around on the floor with the other. They were both free-range, as all our pets were when I was growing up, and one night they disappeared together. To which heaven? I know this: if Lulu consented to go to the dog one, Tubby has her back.

I would also like to see Stranger, with regard to whom I have a recurring pang. Stranger was an unaltered tabby we had when I was a boy, during a period when for some reason we had no dog. Stranger was his own cat, came and went as he pleased and spent more time gone than back. I assumed that the relationship between Stranger and me was mutually satisfactory as follows:

"'Lo, Stranger."

"'Lo, Roy."

"Want a little scratch between the ears?"

"Catch you later."

But then, while we were visiting my grandparents in Jacksonville, Florida, I came down with chicken pox so bad they thought for a while it was smallpox, and to make me feel better my parents got me a puppy: Bobby, a shaggy nondescript who did not turn out to be that great a dog, as a matter of fact, but hey, he was a puppy, he was my puppy, and I came home with him in my arms. Stranger, hovering around the home place, jumped out at me . . .

And saw that puppy, and drew back.

"Oh, Stranger's heart is broken," my mother said. Stranger had missed me, had shown his feelings, and how had I repaid him? With someone new and cuddlier.

Now that was as much my mother's perception as it was Stranger's. But if Stranger actually wasn't as impressionable as all that, I was, and it's a moment I still haven't gotten over. Certainly I never expected Bobby to usurp Stranger . . .

But I did hurt a good cat's feelings. You might think cats aren't creatures of sentiment, but that's where you'd be wrong. They just don't wear their feelings on their sleeves.

Dogs, clearly, wish they could talk. Not if it would mean giving up rolling in decaying animal matter, no. But you can tell by the way dogs look at you—there are times when they crave to put things into words. For instance, all those times when we had to go find Bobby at the pound because he'd wandered off and been picked up by the dogcatcher— maybe he'd been drinking, I don't know. He'd be lying there on the concrete floor in a heap with several really down-and-out-looking dogs, and he'd perk up when he saw us, my mother and me, but there was always some kind of issue there that he was willing to acknowledge, apparently, from the look on his face, but we could never tell what it was. Conceivably, he was trying to say, "It was Stranger! He got me drunk!"

Cats, on the other hand, might not want to bother with words. Cats over the years have given me a wide range of looks: affable, dismissive, wary, indulgent, pouty, analytical, flirty, sportive, indignant, provocative. Never has a cat looked at me as if to say, "What I wouldn't give, if only I could get *through* to you . . ." I have glanced over my shoulder and caught cats looking more intently, even more sympathetically, at the back of my head (which, to be fair, probably looks more like a cat) than at the front.

A cat, otherwise immobile and its eyes closed, will scan a circulating person around the room with its ears, first one and then the other. But that doesn't make a cat, in human terms, "a good listener." A cat tunes in on a need-to-know basis. And when a cat has something it needs to convey, the cat is like a duchess in Timbuktu who registers her wishes in louder and louder English. Humans have the expression "in no uncertain terms." To a cat, this goes without saying. It may be that everything goes without saying, to cats.

But does this keep us from having conversations with cats? By no means. They look sort of like houris and sort of like magistrates: we want to present ourselves to them in the best possible light. And we do sense that they respond, in their fashion. Given sufficient access and inclination, a cat will reach out and touch, with its paw, a person's nose.

The question arises, what kind of meter should cat poetry be in? Perhaps, given that cats have four quiet feet, they should write in little-cat-feet tetrameter. I once sang, as a guest on *A Prairie Home Companion*, a song that a particularly deliberate cat might sing, one syllable per foot, to the tune of "My Dog Has Fleas":

I don't like dogs,
Dogs don't like me.
I wish dogs would
Go climb a tree.

If I were big
And dogs were small
Then there would be
No dogs at all.

I'd eat them like
I ate the par-
Akeet that used
To perch up there.

But since dogs have
An edge on size,
I concentrate
On looking wise.

The time will come
When cats take charge.
Then there'll be no
Point being large.

That's all I have
To say, for now,
Except for purrr,
Pfft, and meow.

But maybe cat-verse feet should be more like this:

Cats scratch, dogs fetch.
Dogs catch, cats stretch.

Then, too, although cats are creatures of habit (I know a family whose cat is happy
to go camping with them in the great outdoors, as long as they bring along the kitty
litter), cat verse should not be regular, in the human sense of regular. Maybe it should
be more like this:

Song of a Volatile Lump in the Bed

While you sleep
It pleases me to creep
In alongside you for a while.
Later, maybe, I'll
Jump up and yowl,
And you'll wake up and scowl
And look at me quizzically.

Here's the deal: physically
You're warm to
Conform to.

But if I get vibes in the night?
I'm a cat, all right?

Maybe that is still too anthropomorphic. Maybe cat verse should wend its way the way a cat does:

I'll get
There how
I get there, when
I
Do. Felines don't
Make
Bee-lines.

I mentioned Mencken before. Mencken showed such an obsessive interest in my computer that I let him go ahead and have at the keyboard once. Here is what he wrote:

Gggggggggggggggggggggggggggggggggggggggggggggggggggggggggggggggggggggggggg
bbbbbbbbbbbbbbbbbbbbbbbbbbbbbbbbbbbbbbbbbbbbbbbbbb

Doesn't look like much, I know, but you should have been there. Cat placed right paw on *g* key, watched the *g*'s stream across the screen for a while, then whapped at the *g*'s on the screen with same paw, which made the *g*'s stop. Came down with both paws on the space bar. Watched cursor move across, making no mark, for a while, then whapped at the cursor, still with one paw on the space bar so didn't stop it. Whapped again. All the *g*'s disappeared as the cursor went spacing off into infinity. Cat jumped at screen with both feet, which did stop the cursor. Cat came down on the *b* key with one foot. That transported us back under the line of *g*'s and started producing a stream of *b*'s. Cat violently attacked screen with both feet. That stopped the *b*'s. It was Microsoft Word, incidentally, that insisted on turning the first *g* into a capital. Computers and cats might keep each other occupied for extended periods.

It wouldn't be poetry, to any of our senses. Perhaps that is what a cat does for the household: reminds the rest of us not to be too quick to assume, either inclusively or exclusively, what constitutes "our." Here is what a French cat might write, on hearing his person refer to him possessively:

> *"Mon chat"? "Mon"?*
> *Chat a toi?*
> *Non.*
> Le *chat, c'est moi.*

But this is just noodling. We don't believe a cat is speaking, in any language, unless we can visualize the cat. For the naked eye, cats are a great subject—now resembling a beanbag, now a bundle of live wires in a velvet sleeve. Posing is natural to them; they pose when they're bathing, they pose in their sleep. But cats have heard somewhere that cameras steal your soul. We know this from family photos. Cats will vanish, or struggle, or they will go all rigid and staring, or they will blur themselves by means of some inner countevibe. Cats and flashbulbs should not be spoken of in the same breath.

Valerie Shaff, as she has shown in our previous books together, is without peer at capturing the facial expressions of dogs, and cows, and ducks. But dogs, cows, and ducks are so available, emotionally. Whereas cats withhold. The more noncommittal the Sphinx grows with age, the more it resembles a cat. But one night there was a soft knock on Valerie's door. Very low down. She opened the door, cautiously, and saw a muffled diminutive figure, face shrouded by a heavy, hooded cloak. It handed her a note, and then was gone. The note said, "Remember Natasha."

And Valerie did remember: the first photograph she ever took of an animal was a headshot, close in, of her cat Natasha, which she framed and gave to her father when she was sixteen.

"All right, then, it's cats!" she cried, and she proceeded to access—as you can see in this book—the essence of cat after cat after cat.

Which is not to say Pepe will like this one either.

I am the cat, don't forget that

I'm a cat,

Can't you see?

You can't get

Over on me.

I'm out of here, boss—
Strange vibes in that thing.
The keys are good to walk across,
But wires aren't a cat thing.

Windows are closed now
Indoor aromas ripen
Mice are seeking warmth

—Haiku

So this is "Outside."

It sure is wide.

Okay, I acknowledge in a higher power.

Now let that liver a little lower . . .

Domestic? Sometimes. Sometimes savage.

It's up to you, to work out the av'age.

I like you personally, sure,
But I *belong* to the furniture.

Oh, jeez, my stalker.

He thinks I'm his personal treat.

He—*ooo*—gets me going. Then . . .

Licks his own feet.

"Eat that," you say, "that's good!"
Tell a cat about a cat's food.
You want to know what's good?
Rat's blood.

Hmm? Why? Well, the challenge—
Note the use of tail for balance—
And it makes my feet feel . . .
What's the big deal?

I've told you, and told

You, this is not a frown.

I'm a Scottish Fold.

My ears turn down.

Ah, the lives that I've been through,
The lofty and the mean.
A slave girl made to dance . . . Then too,
A gem-laden queen.

The aches of passion and duty,
The grand processions, the wars.
It's all there if you look, the beauty
Of course, and the scars.

My name is Scooby. My sister: Dooby.

Yes, we're close. Wouldn't you be?

I'm a little bitty kitten, and

Independent of the litter, and

MAAAAAAA!

At the risk of seeming unkind . . .
You live here in the city too?
Isn't there someone else you can find
To go "Kitty-kitty" to?

Have you ever seen anything whiter than me?

I am as white as a being can be.

And fluffy, am I? And beautiful? Very.

And by the way I just ate the canary.

"I want to rock you," Tom moans,

"Till your back ain't got no bones."

"Hush," I purr, "it can never be.

I'm on the sofa, you're in a tree."

Frankly I'm astonished you would put it like that.

Don't you know "Just do it" doesn't do it for a cat?

Yes, I knocked over

The candelabrum.

And now I'm on the sofa.

What is the problem?

Texture like the sound of purr:

Rough tongue on smooth fur.

Shifting from sixth sense into seventh . . .

Whoa! I think I hit eleventh.

I can tell what you are thinking—

You think

I don't blink.

Maybe I blink while you are blinking.

That bird? They think they shot it?

I got it.

I could *be* a bird

If I preferred.

I'm Satan or satin—which?

Watch me switch.

You're aware, are you not,

How uncool it would be if we fought?

That's what I thought.

No doubt you're
   Hoping I'll purr.
But I'm demure
   And must demur.

You see before you no mere cat:

Madam Lady of the Bathroom Mat.

I've heard people
Say they can't sleep.
Can't *sleep?*
Oh, please.

What do we do when you're not here?

This will give you some idea.

Higher animal, are you, Miss?

Do this.

The yawning relaxes, the stalking tones,

But in the end it's all in the bones.

Front left, back right, and three, and turn . . .
Cats know steps you'll never learn.

Okay I jumped up on that first shelf—

Plinkyplinkplinkplink—

And now find myself

Here. Got . . . to . . . think . . .

For someone with no vibrissae
You're awfully touchy, Missy.

Just a moment, please,

I'm busy eating these . . .

What do you call these. Flowers?

Your flowers?

Ours.

Is *that* what you want of me?

I'm telling you nice:

Whatever the economy,

I don't chase mice.

Where do I go

When I'm out all night?

You don't really want to know,

All right?

A chill: They've turned on
"Air-conditioning." I'll eat
The philodendron.

—Haiku

Since you've come to the shelter,
Surely you've felt a
Need to free
Me?

I know a little place called Doo-wah Ditty!

Whoops! Whoops! Craaaaazy kitty!

An outing. Interesting, yes.
But I belong at my address.

When I purr
Don't infer
It's because you pat.

No, you pat
Because I purr.

I am the cat,
Don't forget that.

Hurrah, the hero airman with his muffler and his hat!

(He'd never have gotten off the ground without his hero cat.)

So you're involved in your "work," yes, dear—
This thing here, and this and that.
Your "papers," and—no, that's not a mouse, dear—
Relax. I have it all covered. Let's chat.

"Three little kittens . . ."

Like us? Oh, what will they do?

Wait . . . What's "mittens"?

And who the hell are you?

A town like this—hello, Mrs. Dunn—
Everyone knows you, you know everyone.

You've caught all the mice.
Twice.

I am a Leo,
And you? A Libra?
Balancing. Me? Oh,
Stalking a zebra.

Here I am in the wilderness.

I'll be spitting at wolves I guess.

I have been a kitten,
Romping all day.
I have been a tomcat, smitten
In the worst way.

Now I'm an old cat.

How about that.

By the sea, by the sea,
By the beautiful sea . . .

What's that? You say
This is not the sea?
I see. Thank you.

By the sea, by the sea,
By the beautiful sea . . .

Indeed I am a wonder,
But deep down under
All this beauty, there's—
Oh, who cares?

Want to know the secret of the shape I'm in?

As a cat I am always at home in my skin.

When I itch, I get right *at* it, natch:

No place on a cat that a cat can't scratch.